Hurricane Dancing

Hurricane Dancing
Glimpses of Life with an Autistic Child

D. Alison Watt

Photographs by Carole Ruth Fields

Jessica Kingsley Publishers
London and Philadelphia

The right of D. Alison Watt to be identified as author of this work has been asserted by her in accordance with the Copyright, Designs and Patents Act 1988.

First published in 2004
by Jessica Kingsley Publishers
116 Pentonville Road
London N1 9JB, UK
and
400 Market Street, Suite 400
Philadelphia, PA 19106, USA

www.jkp.com

Copyright © D. Alison Watt 2005
Photographs copyright © Carole Ruth Fields 2005

Library of Congress Cataloging in Publication Data

Watt, D. Alison (Dawn Alison), 1961-
Hurricane dancing : glimpses of life with an autistic child / D. Alison Watt ; photographs by Carole Ruth Fields.
p. cm.
ISBN 1-84310-792-9 (hardcover)
1. Autistic children—Poetry. I. Fields, Carole Ruth. II. Title.
PS3623.A875H87 2005
811'.6—dc22

2004013527

British Library Cataloguing in Publication Data
A CIP catalogue record for this book is available from the British Library

ISBN 1 84310 792 9

Printed and Bound in Great Britain by
Athenaeum Press, Gateshead, Tyne and Wear

To Steve
for sharing the storms
and daring to dance

You have turned for me
my mourning into dancing.

Psalm 30:11

ACKNOWLEDGEMENTS

Thank you to Jessica Kingsley Publishers for embracing this project and to my editor, Sandra Patruno. Thank you, Carole Ruth Fields, for your sensitive view through photographic lenses. Thank you, Linda Blier, for your endless aid on the journey toward publication. Thank you, Jean Forster, for acting as my agent. Thank you to the North Shore Education Consortium for its talented teachers and expert therapists. Thank you, Dr. Jefferson Prince, for taking such good care of our girl. Thank you, Julie Lambert and the In-Home Support people that have become a part of our family. Thank you to our parents, siblings and friends for your constant support in both big and small ways. Thank you, Steve, for your skill in editing and for believing.

Thank you, God, for the gift of expression. Thank you, Alexa, for making me a better person. You taught me the truth about love.

Contents

Preface

For many weeks Rick Warren's *The Purpose Driven Life* has been at the top of *The New York Times* 'Best-Seller List'. Clearly, part of our human experience is longing for purpose and meaning both in our daily lives and in our life's work as a whole.

I remember contemplating the purpose of my life after I got married and moved to Massachusetts. For all my seeking about job choices and career directions an answer was starting to reveal itself deep inside my soul. It is hard to explain but I knew with growing certainty that one of the purposes in my life would involve a child. It was as if God was saying to me, "I have a job for you to do. Take care of this child." Then when our daughter was born, I began to see what a job it was.

By some unspoken agreement somewhere as soon as you enter the world of special needs children, you are given Emily Perl Kingsley's poem entitled "Welcome to Holland". We were given multiple copies. It describes how if you thought you were going to Italy but end up in Holland instead, it is disappointing but it will be all right. It is just *different*. But nowhere in that poem does it hint at the difficulty found in "different". The behavior issues that sometimes accompany autism take expertise, long struggling work and, at times, just holding on with both hands to your waning sanity. My husband and I have experienced being at the brink of divorce and in the throes of depression. We, like most parents of special needs children, have felt isolated from other families because of the severe limitations of ours. "No, we cannot go to that theme park on Spring Break", "No, we cannot fly on an airplane right now", "No, we cannot meet you at the restaurant." We can't even wait in a line. Maybe next year. Always the hope and hard work toward next year.

So, we are on this different path which we did not choose. There is a time to research and educate ourselves about therapies and treatments; there is a time to fight systems and bring awareness in order to make a way for our child to belong; but there is also a time to reflect, to breathe. Most of the poems in this collection were born from intense and sometimes traumatic incidents with our child. Some of the experiences and emotions were too hard to process without working them out on paper and they came out in my native tongue: poetry.

Reflection is healing. It allows us to draw strength from beyond ourselves. It helps us recognize and experience love in such a pure form, we cannot help but sense the Divine. This kind of love is more learned than instantly accepted or achieved. It demands sacrifice but does not diminish sadness. It is stronger than we are and will not die. It finds a different language if it has to.

I found out about the importance of this kind of love when we last flew with Alexa. I was sitting with her in the early morning hours at Detroit Metro waiting for Steve to check our bags. Actually, I was sitting and Alexa was dancing and running around a bit. Often, she would come over and fling her arms around me and we would laugh and snuggle. I was just grateful she was being good. I noticed that a woman had come to sit near us. What I did not notice was that she was watching. After a while Steve was coming back to claim his family and I stood up. This woman suddenly ran toward me and cried, "I have to hug you!" I hugged her and then pulled away to look into her face. "Do I know you?" I asked, thinking I must. "No", she answered with tears trickling down her face, "but I have to hug you again." I did not understand. She quickly explained. Her daughter was recently in a car crash. She suffered a brain injury and was mentally impaired. The daughter that they knew was gone and this mother was now trapped within the impassable walls of grief. But watching Alexa and me gave her hope. She kept repeating to me, "I get it now! I am going to be OK!" I was so humbled that Alexa and I could unknowingly pass on such a powerful and essential thing as hope. This woman could see the love between us. It had a different face and a different future, but it was there. And she got it. Like all parents and caregivers who let God guide them along a different, even difficult path, she was going to be OK.

In The Morning
1997

I heard a mother say
she dreamed her child
could talk with her
and tears flowed
from unopened eyes
in the morning.

I awakened with
unaccustomed weight,
wishing the wrong away
and dreading forever's
first thought
in the morning.

Small arms embraced my neck
bright eyes willed mine
to open
and courage spoke
love's words
in the morning.

Adrienne

1997

Solemn soul
haunting beauty
hair spun by
sunlight's gold.
I felt awe
in meeting you.
Suddenly, you were there
watching silently
as I came closer.
Wandering one—
you led me
into your room,
your life.
I watched, entranced
by your spirit-ways.

> You touched the shoulder
> of each friend playing
> and with your thumb
> signaled back toward me.

"She's introducing you,"
your mother whispered.
I could not have been
more honored
if I'd traveled
through the twilight
and spoken
to a star.

Playground Prayer
1998

Playgrounds are a stage
of isolation.
I stand alone
set apart
different
because my daughter is.
I watch her trying
to catch some child's eye.
Hers, positively dancing in playfulness
wordlessly wondering if one
would chase her up the slide.
I shower silent blessings
on the child who is willing
to answer playground prayers
and end this aching vigil
with "hello."

Hurricane Hard
1997

When you hear me
talking about what it's like
to have an autistic daughter,
Tell me "Wow,
that must really be something."
Tell me you admire the kind of
mother I've become.
Tell me you can't imagine it
(although you could if you'd try).
Tell me "You go girl,
loving and raising that child."
Tell me anything
but for God's sake
don't tell me
you're sorry,
even if you mean that you're sorry
you have it easier and I have it hard.
Shoot.
Easy is the intricate patterns of the brain
effortlessly connecting so mind and voice
come together in order to utter
an appropriate word
earning an acknowledging smile
and a story to tell Grandma.

Hard is getting a pair of blue eyes
that tend to flicker off your face
faster than a flame
ignited by an old lighter
to hold steady,
look at your mouth,
and watch you form the word.
Waiting days, then weeks, then months
to see her begin to understand
you have a name.
Hard is believing without seeing the hope
you defend with every drop of blood
that pulses from your heart
throughout your body
that she will someday use that name
to call you.
Hard is hearing it, finally
and having heaven fall on your face
resting with relief under a ray of warmth
from an assertive sun that shines regardless
of what lies in the way.

It's like getting your best dress soaked
dancing in the wild rain
learning to laugh at the back
of a hurricane.

Big Bus Hang-Up

1997

I don't have a big bus hang-up.
Special Ed vans have picked her up
since age three.

I don't look at big buses with longing—
A door-to-door drive is OK with me.

I don't have bigger bus issues,
But a lump in my throat arrives every day
As a little bus carries my big love away.

Conversation
1998

"Alexa, today is Saturday.
What do we make for breakfast
on Saturday?"
"Pancakes!"

        God bless the determination

"What comes first?"
"Egg!"
"Then what?"
"Flour! Pour some milk!"

        of a Daddy for his daughter

"What's next?"
"Oil!"
"Good job!"
"Stir it up!"

        that as surely as the dawn comes

"Careful—hot! What do you need now?"
"Butter and syrup—
Pancakes, my favorite!"

        she can count on him.

Going "Granny"
1997

I'm learning not to notice
looks some people give
out like flowers
for their Granny
(but really, I'm
the wolf)
in a sort of reversed
role, Red Riding Hood.
"My, what strange sounds she makes!"
"My, what bad behavior!"
My thoughts play up the punch line,
"The better to eat you with, my dear—
GRRR!!!!"
Perhaps the hunter is coming soon,
the straight man and
his jacket,
to take me away
from stares I'm really trying
not to see.

Arrow of Truth
1998

Alexa and I went to inspect
a house with a friend.
The Realtor leaned into the car
with a cheerful "hello" for Alexa
that was far too happy for the kind of hassled
day I was having.
"She's autistic," I grumbled,
slamming the door shut
on expectations of an answer.
My friend shot at me like an arrow
"You don't have to say that!"
She's your daughter first,
then she's autistic.
You love her—
That's all anyone needs to know."
The truth of her words pierced me first
then lent me wings to let go.

Founder's Day in Foxboro

1997

Today we watched a parade
high on life (or Ritalin).
You caught and held
candy in your hand
watching the crazy, waving nonsense
promenading by.
Our mistake to push it.
Going to the field—
overwhelming masses of people
overstimulating senses.
We tried the playground
but you were a wild thing
plowing through kids you didn't even see.
There was a flash of pink dress
and blond hair and a little girl's
crying face running to her mama.
And in my head I told that mama,
"I'm sorry your child is hurt
from a minor infraction of playground rules,
but I'm sorry more for my wounded child
who is pained in deeper ways."
Playground finished,
Time for stroller.
You flung yourself on the sand.
Three times we tried to pick you up
and put your frantic, twisting body
into the seat of a stroller
that attempts to look sporty
in spite of revealing, restrictive straps.
We couldn't do it.

We just couldn't get you there.
I felt the eyes of all those people
looking at us, wondering, questioning, judging.
Out of breath I whispered,
"Let's lay her down—let her work it out,"
and you writhed on the ground
with your lip bleeding and your knees scratched
screaming, screaming until every other noise was
    blocked
and all I saw was you
and all I heard was blood
pulsing too strongly through my ears.

I stroked your head,
startled when a woman nicely asked
if we needed help and could she
get someone.
It struck me as ridiculous then
that I could smile
and say, "No, she's autistic, it's OK,
thank you."
I felt tears surging up from my
blood-rushing heart but I stopped them cold.
We stroked your head
and you blinked up into the sunshine.
We spoke quiet words
that you began to understand.
Then you got up, sat in that stroller
and with my head held high
I pushed you proudly
through the crowd.

Her Eyes
1998

When someone offers to give you a break,
you take it. You relax and enjoy
the luxury of late breakfasting with your husband
and out-of-state friend.

Renewed, you return for your child. She's
    on edge—
you can feel it. It's not the best time to forget
    your purse—
but you do. You know from experience
    that pulling
back into a driveway you've just left, simple as
    it seems,
is enough to send her spinning,
and it does.

Your husband and friend are in the front seats,
    you and your child
are in the back. She is wildly thrashing in the
    throes of frustration. Her screaming keeps
    her from hearing
your firm instructions and the growing silence of
    your friend.
Your child is pulling you painfully by the hair
into her battle, but the patience you've
    developed helps you
refuse to engage. You lift your hands in
    self-protection.

Inside part of you laughs a little. You think, "This
    is absurd,
I'm being beaten by a 5-year-old."

Then of all things, you have to get her out
    of one car
and into another. You and your husband
    take action,
a well-trained team in synchronized support.

You know you can face this storm
of unmerited fury. You know her
crazed, frightened eyes will soften again.
You will all be alright. Just don't glance up.
Don't glimpse through the grimy rear window
the sight of your friend standing out of the way,
sobbing.

Later you will explain to her
this awful scene—
the rocky part of a path that will eventually
lead to steadier ground. You are determined
it must. You travel this brokenness with
the finest teachers, doctors, and behaviorists
who share your determination. You know you
must do whatever it takes to reach her.
You know love reaches back in her eyes.

This is Pain
2000

Today at the Laundromat
a man came and stood at the counter with
his little girl
I was checking on our drying clothes
with one eye on Alexa.
I saw her go over to them,
grab at the little girl's hair with thickly
    gloved hands,
and was there in seconds.

I felt the man's anger
as we both struggled to move her away.
I spoke immediately, clearly,
"She's autistic."
"Alexa, gentle hands, hands down."
I inspected the girl—
she did not seem at all upset.
"OK," the man snapped.
I hesitated a moment
wishing, as I always do
for some way to get through to Alexa
some way to teach her about hurting people...

"Will you kindly move please?"
he unkindly said.
Alexa and I stepped away.
"Keep moving—get her away from
my daughter," he growled.
I looked at him, shocked
my thoughts darting wildly in different directions.
Was this merely about a missing barrette
or something distinctly more distasteful?
I offered inadequately,
"She's OK, we're OK."
"Well, I'm not."
"You obviously don't know much about autism,"
 I countered,
my own anger rising.

Then in a voice curdled with sarcasm,
words poured from an outdated carton
hitting my stomach
sour
"Yep, and I'll bet you're a Social Worker."
"I'm her mother!" I gasped.
"Well, you should be a Social Worker
I'm sure you're a very good person," he mocked
without looking at me,
teaching his daughter about hurting people…

I hugged Alexa closer
slowly moving toward the door
biting back defenses
of my wonderful, precious
already-on-five-medications
doesn't-know-what-she's-doing-daughter.
I buckled her into the car
went back in, grabbed baskets
stuffed them full with still-drying clothes
tears unashamedly streaming down my face.

"Oh God, this is pain
I don't want to feel."
This intolerance
This ignorance
This malice.
Two women approached me
offering their choice word descriptions
of the man
"I'm alright," I cried
rushing back to the car.

"But I can't see,
can't breathe.
Oh God, Oh God
this is pain."

Ponderings

2001

Standing in line for ice cream today
I saw two boys
laughing at Alexa
who was waiting in the car.

laughing at Alexa...

I thought,
"This is new. This has
never happened before."
I looked at her and tried to see her
through their eyes.
She looked typical but here was the thing:
she was singing and talking to her self
waving a stick around
in a somewhat frantic fashion
beating up on air.

I didn't blame them
but I did walk over
and tossed a loud, "I love you, Lex!"
through the window
as if those words could somehow
surround the car and protect her from realities
like laughter from little boys.

I haven't told a soul
about what I saw today
not even Steve
I am keeping these things
and, like Mary,
pondering them in my heart.

Sand Castles

1998

I scan the sand for castles
and steer us between
but specks of airborne messengers
call her with a whirlwind whisper
reminding her fingers how it feels
to dig deep into freshly packed sand.
Temptation is a terrible tease
and her mind has not yet learned how
to overrule her senses.
So she runs—we must follow,
rushing to repair.
Boys yell but their claims die—
God's hand in the tide
beat us there.

Sticks and Stones
1997

Most people celebrate milestones.
Mine celebrate every stone
along her way
literally.
She skips and dances
where others walk.
She shouts and sings
when others know to whisper.
She is fascinated
by sticks and stones
while others are preoccupied
by damage.
She teaches me to celebrate
small things beneath
our happy-and-we-know-it
stomping feet.

Joy of Life
1998

I moved through a museum of art
treading softly so I could hear
the thoughts of an artist's mind.
I turned around and saw her
in a sculpture—
the rendering of my child.
From the hardness of bronze
a little girl bounded
dancing in waves
with her arms lifted high
and her face tilted toward the sun.
"Joy of Life" defined
is Alexa.
In brave defiance to difficulty
there is brilliance in her eyes,
music in her voice,
exuberance in her step.
Laughter is the language
of her soul.

Hearing Things

2000

> "Alexa, this is Doug.
> Do you remember our friend
> Doug?
> Say hello to Doug!"

She looked at him then looked at me
downright disbelieving.

He walked away
and to his back
she said hello:
> *"Quack, quack, quack."*

Overcrowding

2001

It's funny how laughter and pain
can show up at the same cocktail party
mingling emotions as if they each
didn't mean more to you than that.

It leads to overcrowding.

Joy, grief, pride, love
all thrown together in the same place—
a heart made of strong brick
and glass windows
where strange rain
reaches in and wets the face of an aging girl

watching her daughter shine
at Circle Time.

Two Shells

2001

Two college kids came for dinner
spilling out statistics
over coffee and dessert.

"Did you know," they asked us,
"that parents of autistic children have the
    highest
rate of divorce?"

Steve and I looked at each other.
Yes. We know.

Often love dies when hit by such a storm.
Let it.
Two shells of a cracked seed separate,
sooner or later fall away—
it's the root that matters.
Once the storm spins itself out,
mist falls and the sun begins to clear a path
persuading a resilient plant
with a most breathtaking flower
to grow.
It still can.

Let it.

Meetings
2001

It was a productive business meeting
I thought
great ideas shared
implementations structured
goals set
profits assured.

We shook hands and smiled
stuffed notes into bulging leather bags
and said goodbye.

Then why did my eyes sting with silly tears
as I walked out to the car?

Oh, yes. I remember.
This business is not my job.
She's my child.

Patience

2001

Every school day morning
as I put Alexa on the bus,
my eyes fall for a moment on Patience.
She sits at the front of the bus in a special seat,
her face is often wet with drool,
she is very, very small.
It seems to me that just behind her round
    brown eyes
a smile waits.
Steve said once he saw her wave.

It was Christmastime and the bus driver
surprised me by handing over a gift for Alexa.
"Who is this from?" I asked him.
"Patience," he answered.
I brought it upstairs and sat down with Alexa to
    open it.
Inside the plastic wrapping was a gingerbread
    house for us to decorate,
There were bags of candy and some frosting.
The card said, "To My Friend.
Love, Patience."

I thought about her mother.
I thought about our need to sporadically stab at
    this thing
called "Normal"
to have our children have friends and give gifts
    and if only for the briefest time make us feel a
    part of that world.
I thought about how kind and wonderful she is to
    have reached out to the other children on
    that bus—giving something they might all
    enjoy.
I thought about those cards
lovingly written by one on behalf of another—
mother communicating for her child.
I thought about her longing
and heard my own in our reply,

"To Patience—
Thank You!
Love, Your Friend,
Alexa."

43

Carry You
1999

"Carry you—I want carry you,"
is what Alexa says when she
means "carry me."
It comes from the question
"Do you want me to carry you?"
In true autistic form
an echo is the easiest reply.

She does not understand—
she is taller now
and difficult to carry.
The path of communication
meanders in her mind;
a sparse trail of words
prone to unexpected turns,
hindering the already hard steps of progress.
When her tired and teary eyes plead,
"Carry you—I want carry you,"
my attempts to help her seem painfully
inadequate.

Many times during these
early years of raising Alexa,
I have felt frozen by frustration
captive in a cold, unknown sea.
But my daughter has taught me what to say.
She has given me the words.
I close my weary eyes
and whisper,
"Carry you—I want carry you."
A great big God lifts me up—
lifts us all—and answers
"I AM".

What She Sees
2001

Alexa sees things that I don't.
When we walk into a room
a thousand tiny details bombard her eyes
rushing forward for attention.
And there I stand a simpleton,
trying to pull her
toward hello.

Occasionally she tells me what she sees.
Commenting on objects is a goal
I am sure, listed somewhere among the piles
of task-oriented papers at school.

This I will never forget:
driving on a country road, slowly rounding a lazy curve
not a living soul in my sight—
there was in hers.
Looking out her window, she suddenly, clearly, and
matter-of-factly said,
"angels!"

Of course, I looked.
I didn't see a thing but didn't doubt it either.

Sometimes I get shivers when I think of what she sees.

Work of Angels
1998

There are people who pray for Alexa
everyday of their lives.
A little girl called Claire,
Norma and Ilene, Nikki and Irene,
her Grandparents
to name a few.
I will never underestimate the effect
of their prayers or diminish the power
of believing.

Dan is an 11-year-old boy who came to our
     door the other day
"Is Alexa here? Can Alexa play?"
These are the questions of typical childhoods
I do not have the chance to take for granted.
But the "Dans" in her life touch deeper
than kids being kids ever could.

Letting her call him Tony or Dave,
shooting baskets beside her,
giving her skateboard rides,
he joins Claire and others like her
taking up the work of angels
without wings
helping her fly.